VIRTUAL HISTORY TOURS

Look around a

MEDIEVAL
CASTLE

Clare Hibbert

ARCTURUS

This edition first published by Arcturus Publishing
Distributed by Black Rabbit Books
123 South Broad Street
Mankato
Minnesota MN 56001

Copyright © 2008 Arcturus Publishing Limited

Printed in China

Library of Congress Cataloging-in-Publication Data
Hibbert, Clare, 1970-
  Look around a medieval castle / by Clare Hibbert.
      p. cm. -- (Virtual history tours)
Includes index.
ISBN 978-1-84193-724-3 (alk. paper)
1. Castles--Europe--History--To 1500.
2. Military history, Medieval.
3. Military history, Medieval.
4. Middle Ages. I. Title.

GT3550.H53 2007
940.1--dc22

                    2007007560

9 8 7 6 5 4 3 2

Series concept: Alex Woolf
Editor and picture researcher: Alex Woolf
Designer: Ian Winton
Plan artwork: Phil Gleaves
Consultant: David Nicolle

Picture credits:
Art Archive: 6 (Manuel Cohen), 9 (Dagli Orti), 10 (Real Biblioteca de lo Escorial / Dagli Orti), 12 (Manuel
Cohen), 13 (Castel d'Avio Verona / Dagli Oti [A]), 15 (Biblioteca Nazionale Marciana Venice / Dagli Orti [A]),
16 (British Library), 20 (Dagli Orti), 21 (Musée de la Tapisserie Bayeux / Dagli Orti), 22 (Manuel Cohen), 23,
24 (Dagli Orti), 26 (Manuel Cohen), 28 (Dagli Orti), 29 (National Museum of Sculpture, Valladolid / Dagli
Orti [A]).
Bridgeman Art Library: 18 (Bibliothèque Nationale, Paris), 19 (Singleton Open Air Museum, West Sussex), 25
(Biblioteca Marciana, Venice), 27 (Bibliothèque Nationale, Paris).
Corbis: 7 (John and Lisa Merrill), 14 (Elio Ciol).
David Nicolle: 8.
Arcturus Publishing Ltd: 4, 11, 17.

CONTENTS

Author's note

In this book, you will tour the medieval castle of Krak des Chevaliers as it was in 1270. Some of the stops on your tour involve guesswork: experts are fairly sure there was a hospital on-site, for example, but they have only been able to guess at its most likely position. Of course, some of the features that a 21st-century tourist might see had not yet been built in 1270. The castle underwent more rebuilding after its capture by the Mamluk sultan Baybars, who installed Turkish baths, for example, and converted the chapel to a mosque.

CRUSADERS' CASTLE

Welcome to your tour of a medieval castle. The castle you will be exploring is the Krak des Chevaliers, or "fortress of the knights." The year is 1270, during the era of the Crusades. The Crusades were a series of military expeditions made by European Christian knights to retake the Holy Land from Muslim forces. The Krak is situated in the Holy Land, in the present-day country of Syria. Originally an Arab fortress, the Krak has become the headquarters of a holy order of knights called the Knights Hospitalers.

The age of castles

The Middle Ages was the great era of castle building. Between 1000 CE and 1500 CE, more than 15,000 castles were built across Europe and the Middle East. Kings, princes, and lords lived in these strongholds, safe from enemy attack. After all, the Middle Ages was an unsettled period of history. Countless wars were fought, some in the name of religion, to secure territory and power.

All sorts of fortresses

Castles were built in a variety of styles, depending on the local materials and terrain, but they all shared certain features. They had thick walls and other defenses to keep enemies at bay. There were arms stores and stables, kitchens and living quarters. The finest rooms were the great hall, where knights could meet or eat, and the beautiful chapel.

GREAT HALL: SEE PAGES 22–23
CHAPEL: SEE PAGES 26–27

The Knights Hospitalers were easy to identify on the battlefield in their black surcoats (tunics) with a white cross.

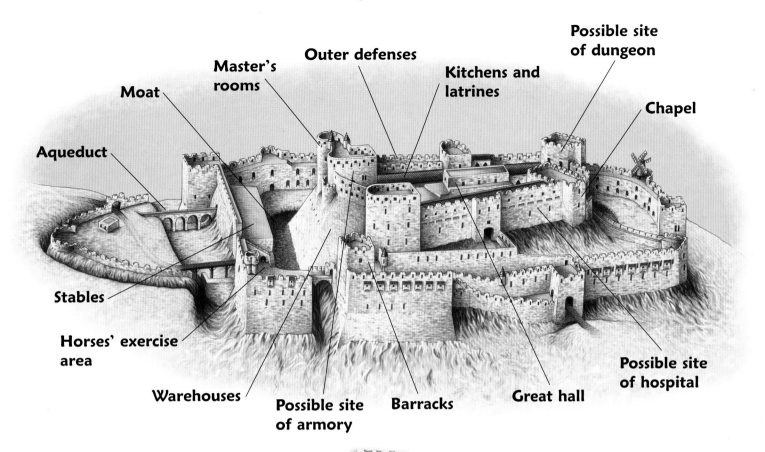

Aqueduct

Moat

Master's rooms

Outer defenses

Kitchens and latrines

Possible site of dungeon

Chapel

Stables

Horses' exercise area

Warehouses

Possible site of armory

Barracks

Great hall

Possible site of hospital

Your tour of the castle will take you to all the areas shown on this plan.

Holy knights

The Knights Hospitalers grew powerful during the Crusades. In their heyday, they owned about 140 citadels in the Holy Land. They dedicated themselves to two tasks: providing armed escorts for Christian pilgrims to the Holy Land and tending the sick (hence the name "Hospitalers"). They also rebuilt the Krak, making it one of the greatest fortresses in the world.

Many different kinds of people went on crusades, according to this anonymous chronicler from Würzburg:

[Some] went in order to learn about new lands. . . . There were others who were oppressed by debts to other men or who sought to escape the service due to their lords, or who were even awaiting the punishment merited by their shameful deeds. . . . A few could, with difficulty, be found . . . who were directed by a holy and wholesome purpose, and who were kindled by love of the divine majesty to fight earnestly and even to shed their blood for the holy of holies.

Annales Herbipolenses, MGH SS XVI. Dated 1147 CE

OUTER DEFENSES

From a dusty track northeast of Tell Kalakh, you catch your first glimpse of the Krak des Chevaliers, a rugged limestone fortress perched 2,300 feet (700 m) above sea level. It's easy to see how this imposing castle withstood sieges from some of the most fearsome forces of the Middle Ages. Its thick outer wall, dotted with towers, was virtually indestructible!

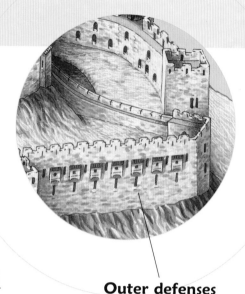

Outer defenses

Withstanding attack

Before the days of gunpowder, cannons, and bombs, fortress walls were hard to breach. The deadliest weapons available to a besieging army were catapults that fired rocks. One type, the trebuchet, was worked by a heavy counterweight. Another, the mangonel, was powered by taut, twisted ropes. Attacking forces also used scaling ladders to climb over the high walls and a battering ram to splinter the castle gate. The ram—a huge tree trunk—was mounted on wheels.

The Krak's main entrance was on the eastern side. This is the western side, with its four round guard towers. Narrow walkways ran along the tops of the walls.

Forces of nature

Castle architects designed their fortresses to withstand attack. The Hospitalers built their outer wall 100 feet (30 m) thick. This was partly so that missiles could not penetrate it, but also to help the Krak stay standing in an earthquake—two serious tremors had damaged the castle shortly after the Hospitalers took it over.

DEFENSE – SEE PAGE 8

Castle walls had up-and-down edges (or crenellations) that gave archers useful cover. This is Obidos Castle in Portugal.

An unknown chronicler describes a Saracen attack on a Christian castle:

As soon as they see the Turks appear, many trumpets sound and many horns. So many are the Saracen men that I don't know how to count them. Those from within the castle, as best I can number them, are but five hundred. Often do they invoke Saint Vincent that he may be their guarantee and shield and that they may defeat the Turks. The castellan [governor of a castle] spurs on his men and rallies them to charge.

"La Vie de saint Julien" (The Life of Saint Julian the Hospitaler), from the Arsenal ms. 3516, Folio 84, dated c. 1286

Wall design

Most medieval castles, including the Krak, had crenellated walls. This meant they had gaps along the top called crenels for archers to fire through, interspersed with raised sections called merlons, which sheltered the defenders from enemy fire. Archers positioned themselves along the long wall walks. Lower down there were narrow slits through which more defenders could fire. Sentries manned the guard towers. The main entrance tower had a wooden drawbridge that was pulled up if the castle was under attack.

MOAT AND AQUEDUCT

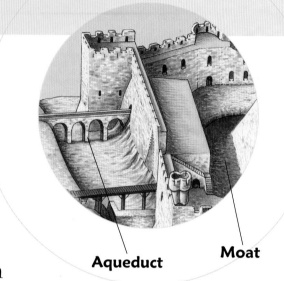

Aqueduct   Moat

Before you enter the citadel, pause on its southern side by a triangular-shaped fortification called an outwork. Here an arched bridge disappears beyond the outer wall. Now walk around to the eastern entrance tower and go in. Scramble through the dog-legged corridors until you're back on the southern side—but inside the castle walls. See how the moat widens to become a deep, rectangular reservoir.

Defense

Moats were an important part of the defenses of many medieval castles. They prevented enemy forces from getting too close to the walls during a siege. The Krak des Chevaliers' moat was dug between the outer and inner walls as an extra barrier between invaders and the inner stronghold. The moat did not completely encircle the castle, however. Not all castles had moats. Some relied on natural defenses. Coastal castles, for example, might be protected on one side by sheer cliffs dropping down to the sea.

The Krak's moat, between the outer and inner walls, was more important as a water store than as a means of defense.

CASTLE DEFENSES: SEE PAGES 6–7

Supplies

The moat and reservoir were an important water supply for the Krak's knights and other inhabitants, including the horses. At some castles, people raised freshwater fish such as carp and perch in the muddy moat waters, which were eventually served up on the table of the great hall. At the Krak, this was not necessary since the knights controlled the fishing in Lake Homs, to the east.

GREAT HALL: SEE PAGES 22–23

A limestone aqueduct carried water into the castle compound. The Krak had wells too and tanks for collecting rainwater.

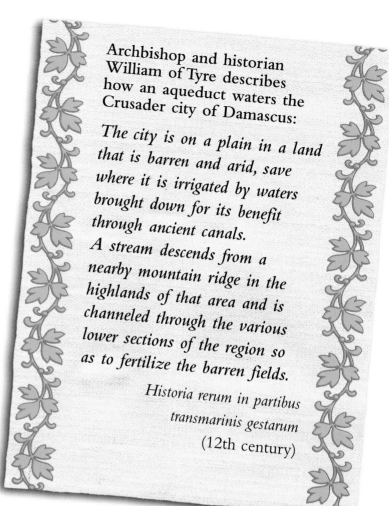

Archbishop and historian William of Tyre describes how an aqueduct waters the Crusader city of Damascus:

The city is on a plain in a land that is barren and arid, save where it is irrigated by waters brought down for its benefit through ancient canals.
A stream descends from a nearby mountain ridge in the highlands of that area and is channeled through the various lower sections of the region so as to fertilize the barren fields.

Historia rerum in partibus transmarinis gestarum
(12th century)

Aqueducts

The Krak's moat was fed by an aqueduct—a water-carrying bridge, supported on arches—that channeled rain and water from high in the hills. Aqueducts were invented by the ancient Romans, who were skilled engineers. During a siege, the knights blocked off the aqueduct so that the enemy force could not poison the water supply. When the reservoir and their underground storage tanks ran dry, the defenders relied on wells within the castle walls.

STABLES AND EXERCISE YARD

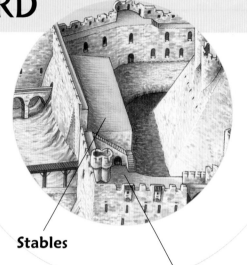

Built into the wall by the reservoir is a huge outbuilding. The stench hits you before you even go inside. This is the castle's main stables. Horses snort impatiently and jostle for space. Most days, but not all, the grooms lead them out to the exercise yard—a patch of bare, trampled earth beside the moat. You passed more stabling on your way into the castle too: the Krak houses hundreds of horses!

Stables

Horses' exercise area

Warhorses

Medieval knights paid for their own warhorse and favored big, strong breeds called destriers that could cope with carrying their armored rider into battle—usually a load of up to 300 pounds (135 kg). The rest of the time, knights rode a much smoother, more comfortable mount—a kind of horse known as a palfrey. Stables also housed fast, lean horses called coursers that were used by messengers.

This illustration from a medieval manuscript shows mounted Crusaders in battle. Each warhorse wears body armor and a protective helmet known as a shaffron.

Caring for horses

Most medieval castles had stabling. Grooms mucked out and gave the horses exercise, fresh water, and fodder—hay from local farmers brought in on mule-drawn carts. Horses were kept in the peak of condition: after a knight's sword, his horse was his most treasured possession. Horses even wore their own armor to limit injuries in battle. Equine (horse) armor included chain mail to protect the body and a steel helmet. Some warhorses had pointy nail heads sticking out of their shoes so they could kick or trample enemy foot soldiers to agonizing effect.

ARMOR: SEE PAGES 16–17

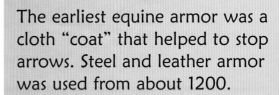

The earliest equine armor was a cloth "coat" that helped to stop arrows. Steel and leather armor was used from about 1200.

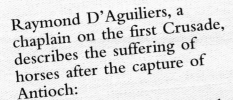

Raymond D'Aguiliers, a chaplain on the first Crusade, describes the suffering of horses after the capture of Antioch:

The poor began to leave, and many rich who feared poverty. If any for love of valor remained in camp, they suffered their horses to waste away by daily hunger. Indeed, straw did not abound, and fodder was so dear that seven or eight solidi [gold coins used as currency in the Byzantine empire] were not sufficient to buy one night's food for a horse. . . .

Fall of Antioch

Rise of cavalry

Horses originally became an important part of warfare thanks to stirrups, a Chinese invention that spread to Europe during the 600s CE. Stirrups made cavalry—soldiers on horseback—effective for the first time because they allowed a knight to brace himself while he delivered a killer blow with his lance or sword.

BARRACKS

You visit one of the three towers along the outer wall that serve as barracks—not for the holy knights, but for the hundreds of foot soldiers recruited from the local countryside and farther afield. Since these men rarely wash, their dormitories don't smell any sweeter than the stables. To help mask the stench, hay, rushes, or scented herbs have been scattered on the floor.

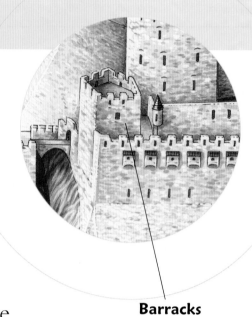

Barracks

Sleeping on straw

Everyone's living quarters were rough and ready in the Middle Ages, but those lowest down the social scale, such as peasants and soldiers, suffered the worst conditions. The barracks at the Krak were in dark, stuffy towers with tiny windows. The men slept on mats or rough straw mattresses. They did not need wardrobes because they had no spare clothes. With careful mending, their cloaks, tunics, and stockings lasted for years.

This is one of the barracks towers at the Krak. The small windows, designed to keep out attackers' arrows, did not let in much light or fresh air.

A soldier's life

Many medieval soldiers were mercenaries—professional fighters who were paid for their services. It made sense for them to sleep near to the guard towers and other posts. Some castles had mess kitchens just for their soldiers. At the Krak, the men made their way into the inner castle to eat in the refectory. Very few medieval castles had large, permanent garrisons like the Krak's; instead they were defended by a few knights and their servants.

Refugees

Whenever a castle was besieged, its population was swelled by local villagers seeking refuge. This could put a terrible strain on the castle's food and water supplies. At the Krak, villagers may have put up tents or simple lean-tos in the space between the outer and inner walls. Disease would have spread fast in these conditions.

Parasites were common in sleeping quarters. Here a Parisian merchant offers advice on catching fleas:

I have heard tell that if you have at night one or two trenchers [of bread] slimed with glue or turpentine and set about the room, with a lighted candle in the midst of each trencher, [fleas] will come and be stuck thereto. The other way that I have tried and 'tis true: take a rough cloth and spread it about your room and over your bed, and all the fleas that shall hop thereon will be caught. . . .

The Goodman of Paris, 1392

FOOD SUPPLIES:
SEE PAGES 14–15

This fresco shows a row of helmeted archers, perhaps mercenaries, preparing to fire. It was painted in about 1350 on a wall at Avio Castle, just north of Verona, Italy.

WAREHOUSES

Warehouses

A ditch surrounds the inner castle, which is built on a high, rocky platform. You scramble along a covered ramp to enter its courtyard. Some of the first rooms you reach are used for storage. Vast areas are needed to shore up supplies so that the castle's inhabitants are able to withstand sieges, which can last for months. One of the Krak's biggest warehouses is about 400 feet (122 m) long.

Provisions

Stored provisions included jars of oil, sacks of grain and flour, and sides of salted meat or fish. Dried or pickled vegetables could be stored too. Herbs and spices were kept to add flavor to foods or to disguise the taste of bad meat. There were barrels of wine, beer, and mead. Some castles kept stores of honey. There was no cane sugar, so honey was an important sweetener. It was also used to treat ailments, so it might have been used in the hospital.

HOSPITAL: SEE PAGES 24–25

At the Krak des Chevaliers, food and other provisions were stored in huge warehouses with low, vaulted ceilings.

Different kinds of mill

One of the storerooms at the Krak des Chevaliers contained an oil mill. Its grinding wheels extracted olive oil, which could be used in cooking, as a lamp fuel, and for anointing the sick. Some castles also had a windmill. The Krak des Chevaliers' windmill was on top of one of its outer-wall towers, where its sails could catch the mountain winds. It produced rye, barley, and wheat flour.

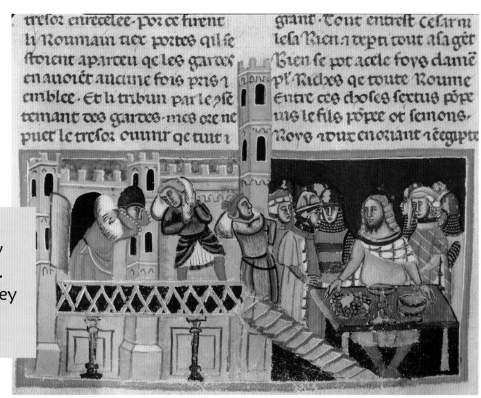

In this 14th-century illumination, soldiers carry sacks of food into a castle. Plentiful stores were the key to surviving a siege.

In a letter to the Archbishop of Cologne in 1197, the Duke of Lorraine describes the capture of the castle at Beirut (in modern Lebanon):

And on the next day following with the army we took the [fortress of Beirut], which was very strongly fortified, without any difficulty. And we found in the fortress so many weapons of arbalisters [crossbowmen] and bowmen that 20 wagons could scarcely carry them, and so many victuals [stores of food] that they were sufficient for 500 men for seven years.

Safe storage

Few castles were as huge as the Krak des Chevaliers, which covered more than 6.9 acres (2.8 hectares), but they all needed most of their cellar space for storage. Water damage or damp could be a serious problem in many castles. At the Krak, the warm climate was more of an issue. The castle steward carried out regular inspections of the stores, but many foodstuffs still became rancid or moldy. Rats plundered the supplies too.

ARMORY

Clang! Clang! Clang! You watch as the castle armorer beats red-hot steel with his hammer. First he heats the metal in the fire to soften it, then he hammers it into shape. It's a skilled job, but it also takes a lot of physical strength. The armory is right at the heart of the castle. Weapons are made, stored, and mended here.

Possible site of armory

The armorer's job

No one can be certain where the Krak des Chevaliers' armory was, but it would have been well protected from the enemy. The armorer made swords, lances, and shields for the knights. He equipped the foot soldiers with daggers, axes, and maces. A mace was about the same length as an ax, but instead of a blade, it had a spiked metal ball. Brought down powerfully enough, it could penetrate metal armor. Foot soldiers sometimes had their own lances or other long pole weapons, such as halberds or pikes.

The Krak's armorer rivets the edge of a helmet while his apprentice stokes the fire. His supplies of iron probably came from Turkey, to the west.

Bows and arrows

The armorer spent a lot of his time fashioning bowstrings and arrows. Craftsmen who specialized in arrow making were known as fletchers. A medieval arrow had a steel tip, a wooden shaft, and some feathers to help its flight.

A Crusader knight wore a long chain mail coat called a hauberk, with a surcoat (tunic) over the top. Armorers made chain mail from rings of thick iron wire that were joined with tiny rivets. It was painstaking work.

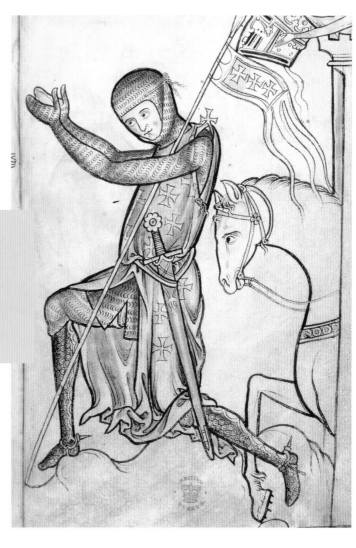

An eyewitness describes how Saladin's archers captured Jerusalem in 1187:

Arrows fell like raindrops, so that one could not show a finger above the ramparts without being hit. There were so many wounded that all the hospitals and physicians in the city were hard put to it just to extract the missiles from their bodies. I myself was wounded in the face by an arrow that struck the bridge of my nose. The wooden shaft has been taken out, but the metal tip has remained there to this day.

De Expugatione Terrae Sanctae per Saladinum (The Capture of the Holy Land by Saladin)

Armor

The armorer supplied knights—and their horses—with armor as well as weapons. Thirteenth-century knights wore a long coat, or hauberk, made of chain mail—thousands of tiny, interlinked, iron-wire rings. Over the top they wore a tunic called a surcoat. The cloth shaded the iron from the sun and prevented it from getting too hot. All the Knights Hospitalers wore a cross on their surcoats. In the 14th century, chain mail was gradually replaced by plate armor. Sheets of solid steel were riveted together to protect every part of the knight's body.

MASTER'S ROOMS

You ascend a spiral staircase to the master's living quarters in one of the three large towers on the south wall of the inner castle. The master is lord of the castle and leader of the Knights Hospitalers. He has a first-floor room for receiving guests or conducting business, then a private chamber above. The two nearest towers are taken up with apartments for the knights. Another of the towers houses the King's Room, where visiting royalty sleeps.

Master's rooms

Furniture

Private chambers were sparsely furnished in the Middle Ages and had few luxuries, even if they belonged to the lord of the castle. They had a big four-poster bed with heavy linen curtains that kept out the drafts and gave the sleeper some privacy. A servant slept in the same room, usually on a pallet or trundle bed that could be stowed beneath the four poster when not in use. A bedchamber might also have a wooden chest for storing clothes and a stool for sitting on.

This picture shows Pierre d'Aubusson, the grand master of the Knights Hospitalers from 1476 to 1503.

Chamber pots and garderobes

There were no flushing toilets in medieval times. Most people kept a chamber pot by the bed. However, some lords had a lavatory, known as a garderobe, built near their chamber. A garderobe was just a stone seat over a hole. Waste could drop down into a cesspit or the moat far below.

MOAT: SEE PAGES 8–9

A 13th-century London clergyman, Richard of Holy Trinity, describes some of the more luxurious spoils of war:

[The captured Turkish caravan] brought mules loaded with spices of different kinds, and of great value; gold and silver; cloaks of silk; purple and scarlet robes, and variously ornamented apparel . . . costly cushions, pavilions, tents . . . chessboards; silver dishes and candlesticks; pepper, cinnamon, sugar, and wax; and other valuables of choice and various kinds. . . .

Itinerary of Richard I and Others to the Holy Land

The feudal system

Medieval society was based on a system known as feudalism. Most castles belonged to a lord. In return for land and other privileges, he served the king and defended him from his enemies. In the same way, a lord gave land to his knights to secure their loyalty. At the bottom of the feudal system were the peasants, who worked the land.

Sitting on a garderobe must have been drafty. Beneath the seat, it was open to the weather.

19

KITCHENS AND LATRINES

Entering the kitchen, you find it is a hive of activity. This is where meals are prepared for the master and all the knights. A cauldron hangs over the top of an open fire. Kitchen boys, or scullions, are performing menial jobs, such as stirring the stew, turning the spit, fetching supplies from the stores, and washing the dirty dishes. Others are cleaning out the latrines at the northern end of the room—there are a dozen of them, side by side!

Kitchens and latrines

Preparing food

Above the scullions were the undercooks. Their jobs included peeling and chopping vegetables, plucking birds, skinning animals, tenderizing the meat, and kneading dough. Most kitchens had a bread oven: the one at the Krak des Chevaliers was 11 feet (5 m) wide. The undercooks answered to the cook. He planned meals, shouted orders, and tasted dishes before they left the kitchen.

Medieval cooks used cast-iron or copper pots like these. This is part of the kitchen at Chateau du Bousquet, a medieval castle in Aquitaine, southwestern France.

Crusader cuisine

Kitchens in Crusader castles produced much spicier food than those in Europe. Cooks used local spices such as sumac, mustard, saffron, cloves, and cinnamon—as well as spices from farther east, such as ginger, nutmeg, and cardamom. Knights who had been on a Crusade helped to introduce Middle Eastern flavorings to western Europe. Cauldron cooking was also borrowed from the Arabs. The big cooking pots were used to make pottage (thick soup), stews, and frumenty (a pudding of wheat boiled in milk).

An Arab diplomat describes a meal shared with a Crusader knight:

We came to the home of a [Frankish] knight who . . . possessed in Antioch an estate on the income of which he lived. The knight presented an excellent table, with food extraordinarily clean and delicious. Seeing me abstaining from food, he said, "Eat, be of good cheer! I never eat Frankish dishes, but I have Egyptian women cooks and never eat except their cooking. Besides, pork never enters my home." I ate, but guardedly, and after that we departed.

Usmah Ibn Munqidh's Autobiography

Two scullions stand on either side of a cauldron, in which meat is slowly stewing over the fire. The image, from the Bayeux Tapestry, dates to the late 11th century.

Kitchen gardens

There is no evidence that the Krak des Chevaliers had a kitchen garden, but most castles did. They had fruit trees, vines, and vegetables. Herbs and other medicinal plants were grown for the hospital. There were also sweet-smelling flowers, used to disguise smells and to decorate the chapel altar. Some castles had a fish pond stocked with trout or pike.

HOSPITAL: SEE PAGES 24–25
CHAPEL: SEE PAGES 26–27

GREAT HALL

Through a vaulted corridor, you reach the great meeting hall, on the western side of the courtyard. It is a grand, imposing room, 89 feet (27 m) long. Here great banquets are served. It is also where knights meet to be briefed on military matters. On one wall, you see a Latin inscription. Translated, it reads "If grace, wisdom, and beauty are given to you, pride alone can tarnish all these qualities when added to them."

Great hall

Medieval meals

In a medieval castle, breakfast was eaten at dawn and consisted of bread and cheese. Dinner, the main meal, began at about ten o'clock in the morning. The evening meal consisted of more bread and cheese and perhaps some soup or stew. In most castles, all these meals took place in the hall. At the Krak, however, the great hall was reserved for banquets, while ordinary meals were taken in a dining hall known as the refectory.

REFECTORY: SEE PAGE 13

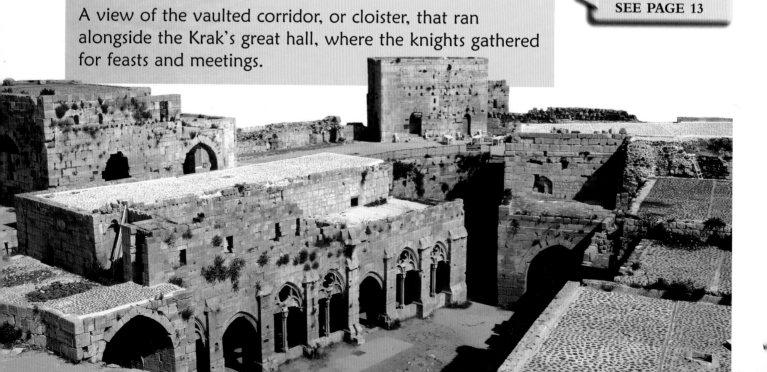

A view of the vaulted corridor, or cloister, that ran alongside the Krak's great hall, where the knights gathered for feasts and meetings.

Dinners and feasts

An ordinary dinner was made up of meat, pastries, bread, fruit, and cheese, washed down with wine or ale. Banquets were far more elaborate. Some consisted of more than 60 dishes! Meats included mutton, beef, ox meat, pork, venison, and hare. Birds ranged from pigeons, capons, and geese to gulls, herons, swans, and peacocks. Fish and shellfish were also served up, along with seals and porpoises. The lord, his lady, and their grandest guests sat on a raised platform. Only those at the high table had plates; everyone else ate their food off a thick slice of stale bread called a trencher.

This 15th-century illumination shows a banquet put on by a noblewoman, who sits at the high table with her honored guests. Trumpets announce the arrival of the food.

English poet William Langland describes changes in the way the rich took their meals:

Woe is in the hall each day in the week.
There the lord and lady like not to sit.
Now every rich man eats by himself
In a private parlour to be rid of poor men,
Or in a chamber with a chimney
And leaves the great hall.

Piers Plowman, 14th century

Entertainments

Some castle halls had a gallery—a high balcony where musicians played or minstrels sang. The harp and lute were common instruments. Dancing was popular by the 13th century. The *estampie* was a couple dance that originated in France in the 11th century. France was also the birthplace of the troubadours, who sang romantic ballads. Other entertainments included acrobats and contortionists.

HOSPITAL

You visit the castle hospital, a long, narrow room lined with rough cots. Here you see Hospitaler monks tending the sick. Some of them are praying with their patients and preparing them for death. Others are administering healing herbs and other painkilling treatments.

Possible site of hospital

Treatments

Plants were used to make medicines and potions. Periwinkle petals brought on vomiting, which was thought to help rid the body of poisons. Artemisia was another purgative and relieved constipation. Primrose leaves were applied to wounds to ease pain. The plant most prized by the Hospitalers was hypericum, or Saint John's wort. It reduced swelling and eased pain.

Few medieval hospitals are still standing. This room, which is 328 feet (100 m) long, is part of the hospital at Tonnerre, France, founded in 1293.

Plagues and epidemics

Dysentery and food poisoning were the biggest killers in the 13th century. More crusading knights died of dysentery than from battle wounds. More long-distance travel between Europe and Asia—by merchants as well as Crusaders and pilgrims—helped to spread disease. The first outbreak of the Black Death (bubonic plague) in Asia was in about 1300. Fifty years later, the Black Death ravaged Europe, killing about 20 million people. Other serious diseases included cholera and typhoid, caused by consuming contaminated food or water.

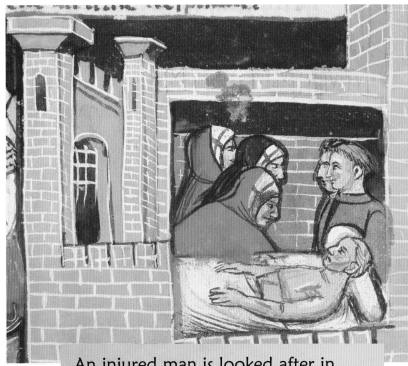

An injured man is looked after in a castle in this 14th-century Italian illumination. Medical knowledge was limited in the Middle Ages, and basic hygiene was poor. Wounds often became infected.

An Arab diplomat describes the healing of an infection:

A horse kicked him in the leg, which was subsequently infected and which opened in 14 different places. Every time one of these cuts would close in one place, another would open in another place. . . . Then came to him a Frankish physician and removed from the leg all the ointments that were on it and began to wash it with very strong vinegar. By this treatment all the cuts were healed and the man became well again.

Usmah Ibn Munqidh's Autobiography

Medieval hospitals

Most hospitals were run by the Church or by holy orders. Although leprosy is not very contagious, it was greatly feared. Lepers had their own hospitals, built away from town centers. Hospitals offered practical care. Medical knowledge was limited but slowly improved during the 12th and 13th centuries. Battle wounds were kept clean and dry for the first time, on the recommendation of a pioneering French surgeon named Henri de Mondeville. Many medical treatments were learned from Arabic practices.

CHAPEL

The chapel stands beside the hospital. One of its outside walls is painted with a beautiful fresco of Jesus as a boy being presented at the Temple in Jerusalem. You go inside. Here the light is dim, but you glimpse more colorful frescoes on the walls. A smell of incense hangs in the air. At the far end, beneath an arched window, you see the altar with its single gold cross. From here, the priest would perform mass.

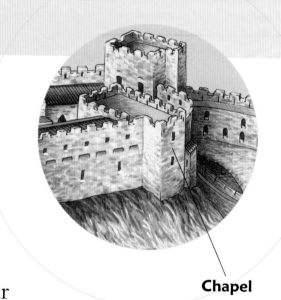

Chapel

From chapel to mosque

Every Christian castle had its chapel. It was often situated high up—as close to God as possible. With its stained-glass windows and painted walls, it was usually the most beautiful room in the castle. The chapel was especially important at the Krak des Chevaliers because the Hospitalers were a holy order. After the Krak fell to Sultan Baybars in 1271, the chapel remained a place of worship. Baybars turned it into a mosque and added a minaret.

This *minbar*, or pulpit, was added after the time of the Knights Hospitalers, when the Krak's chapel was turned into a mosque. From here, the imam delivered sermons and led prayers.

Daily routine

Every medieval castle had its own priest, who led prayers in the chapel. Sometimes he was the only one in the castle who was able to read. He consulted a breviary—a manuscript that set out the daily prayers, hymns, psalms, and other texts. The normal round of prayers consisted of eight prayers at fixed times during the day and another three or four during the night, known as nocturns. The priest also heard confessions and performed blessings. He blessed knights about to go into battle or sick people approaching death.

An eyewitness describes how Muslims took over the Temple of Jerusalem:

The fakihs and kadis [judges], the ministers of the wicked error, who are considered bishops and priests by the Saracens, came for prayer and religious purposes first to the Temple of the Lord, which they call Beithhalla and in which they have great faith for salvation. They believed they were cleansing it and with unclean and horrible bellows they defiled the Temple by shouting with polluted lips the Muslim precept: "Allahu akbar! Allahu akbar!" [God is great.]

De Expugatione Terrae Sanctae per Saladinum (The Capture of the Holy Land by Saladin)

Pilgrims

Pilgrimage was an important feature of medieval Christianity. People went on pilgrimages to demonstrate their faith. The Krak des Chevaliers took in many travelers on their way to or from Jerusalem. Other sites that attracted pilgrims included Rome in Italy and Santiago de Compostela in Spain.

In this 15th-century French illumination, the Knights Hospitalers prepare for battle as a priest says mass in the background.

DUNGEON

Possible site of dungeon

As you've already discovered, much of the Krak is cramped, despite its vast size. Now duck your head and watch your step as you enter the castle's dungeon. Can you imagine what life was like for medieval prisoners? They might spend months or even years in a dark, dank dungeon, with only rats, cockroaches, and other smelly prisoners for company!

French names

Although the word *dungeon* comes from the Norman word *donjon*, which meant the castle's main tower, prison cells were usually underground in the cellars. No one is sure which part of the Krak housed the dungeons. Not all castles had them. Others not only had dungeons but also an *oubliette* (forgotten place)—a secret prison hidden beneath the main cells. Prisoners who were thrown into the *oubliette* were sometimes left to die of starvation.

Stone steps lead down to a torture chamber in the medieval *donjon* at Loches, in central France.

Lords in chains

Many medieval prisoners were nobles. Important hostages were useful when negotiating peace settlements because they could be exchanged for prisoners or lands. They were also useful for raising money in the form of ransoms. When King Richard I of England was captured on crusade, his mother, Eleanor, had to raise a 150,000-mark ransom—the equivalent of two years' income for the king.

This Spanish relief shows gold coins being paid to free a pair of prisoners in chains. Large ransoms could be demanded for important knights.

The 13th-century Cypriot lawyer Philip of Novare describes a settlement:

At last they agreed . . . that he would furnish the emperor with 20 of the most noble vassals of Cyprus as hostages. These men would pledge by their bodies, their belongings, and their estates that the Lord of Beirut would serve the emperor, would go to the court of the Kingdom of Jerusalem, and would there prove his rights, and that, when he had appeared in court, the hostages would be freed and released.

Les Gestes des Ciprois,
The Crusade of Frederick II,
1228–1229

Torture

Some prisoners were captured because they knew about the enemy's battle tactics or long-term plans—or simply because they held different beliefs. Captors used torture to extract information or confessions. Sometimes they used a gruesome device called the rack: it was a wooden frame on rollers that stretched the prisoner and could even pull his arms and legs out of their sockets. Other forms of torture included using splinters of wood to prize off the prisoners' fingernails.

TIMELINE

600	Pope Gregory the Great asks Abbot Probus to build a hospital in Jerusalem.
800s	Feudalism develops in Europe.
1023	Italian merchants rebuild Jerusalem's hospital on the site of the monastery of Saint John the Baptist.
1031	The emir of Aleppo builds a fortress on the site of the Krak.
1066	William of Normandy invades England; the age of Norman castle building begins.
1095	At the Council of Clermont, Pope Urban II calls on the French to take back the Holy Land from the Turks.
1096	The First Crusade begins.
1099	Raymond IV of Toulouse captures the Krak.
c. 1100	The order of Knights Hospitalers is founded in Jerusalem.
1110	Tancred, prince of Galilee, captures the Krak.
1119	The order of Knights Templar is founded.
1123	Saint Bartholomew's Hospital is founded in London.
1144	Raymond II, count of Tripoli, gives the Krak to the Knights Hospitalers.
1186	The Hospitalers buy the fortress of Margat from Bertrand of Antioch.
1187	Saladin recaptures Jerusalem.
1190s	From this time, most castles are built with square towers.
1205	The Hospitalers finish rebuilding the Krak des Chevaliers.
1260	Sultan Baybars founds the Mamluk sultanate.
1268	Sultan Baybars captures Antioch.
1271	Sultan Baybars tricks the Hospitalers and takes control of the Krak.
1272	King Edward I of England sees the castle during the Ninth Crusade.
1270s	The use of machiolations becomes more widespread.
1280s	Edward I, influenced by the Krak, builds his own concentric castles in England and Wales.
1291	The last Crusade ends.
1309	The Knights Hospitalers take control of the island of Rhodes.
1320s	Early cannons appear on the battlefield, giving siege forces the weaponry to topple castle walls.
1400s	Castle building in Europe starts to decline.
1530	The Knights Hospitalers establish themselves on the island of Malta.

GLOSSARY

aqueduct A bridge that carries a waterway.

armorer Someone who makes or supplies weapons and armor.

barracks Sleeping quarters for soldiers.

battering ram A huge wooden beam used to knock down gates.

cesspit A pit dug to hold castle waste and sewage.

chain mail Armor constructed from close-knit iron chains.

concentric castle A castle, such as the Krak des Chevaliers, that has two rings of stone walls.

contortionist A perfomer who can twist his or her body into amazing, unnatural shapes.

crenellated Describing a style of defensive wall that has crenels and merlons.

crenel A gap within a defensive parapet through which archers can fire.

Crusades A series of expeditions by Christian knights who wanted to reclaim the Holy Land from the Muslims.

epidemic A disease that attacks a great many people in one place at a particular time.

feudalism A way of organizing society in which people are given land and other privileges in return for their loyalty.

Frankish Originally describing the Germanic tribes who settled France in the early Middle Ages, the term came to apply to any Crusader knights but especially those from northern France.

garderobe A castle lavatory.

garrison A group of soldiers stationed in a castle or town.

hauberk A long coat made of chain mail.

Holy Land The parts of the Middle East where events described in the Bible took place.

holy order A group of religious people who have been ordained.

machiolation An opening in a projecting structure at the top of a castle wall, used for dropping things onto attackers below.

mangonel A rock-firing catapult, powered by twisted ropes.

mercenary A professional soldier.

merlon A raised section of wall between two crenels, which protects archers from enemy fire.

minstrel A medieval performer who sang and sometimes accompanied himself on a stringed instrument such as a lute.

plate armor Body armor that is made of sections or plates of steel.

pottage Thick soup.

purgative A drug or medicine taken to cause vomiting and emptying of the bowels.

ransom Money paid for the release of someone who is being held prisoner.

scullion A kitchen boy.

siege A military operation in which an army surrounds a castle and cuts off its supplies.

surcoat A cloth tunic worn over a hauberk.

trebuchet A rock-firing catapult, powered by a heavy counterweight.

FURTHER INFORMATION

Books

Biesty, Stephen and Meredith Hooper. *Castles*. Hodder, 2004.

Gravett, Christopher. *Eyewitness: Castle*. Dorling Kindersley, 2000.

Sheehan, Sean. *Medieval World: Castles*. Franklin Watts, 2004.

Smith, A. G. *Cut and Assemble a Crusader Castle in Full Colour: The Krak des Chevaliers in Syria*. Dover Books, 1986.

Steele, Philip. *Best-Ever Book of Castles*. Kingfisher, 1997.

Websites

www.historyforkids.org/learn/medieval/
Links to articles on all aspects of medieval life, including architecture, religion, and food.

www.historyonthenet.com/Medieval_Life/types_of_castle.htm
Different styles of castle building in Britain after the Norman Conquest.

www.knights-of-st-john.co.uk/
A vast resource of articles and images concerning the Hospitalers, including their medieval history but aimed at adult enthusiasts rather than school-age readers.

INDEX

Page numbers in **bold** refer to illustrations.